OWEN DAVEY

BRAINY ABOUT
BEARS

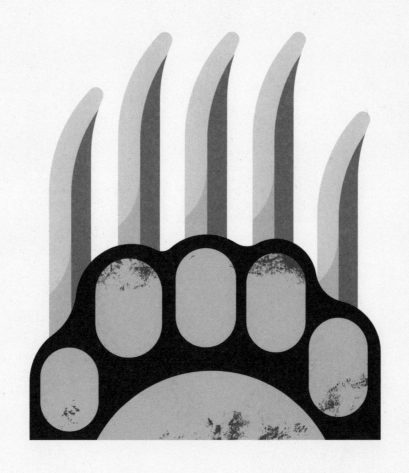

FLYING EYE BOOKS

A brown bear
explores the forest.

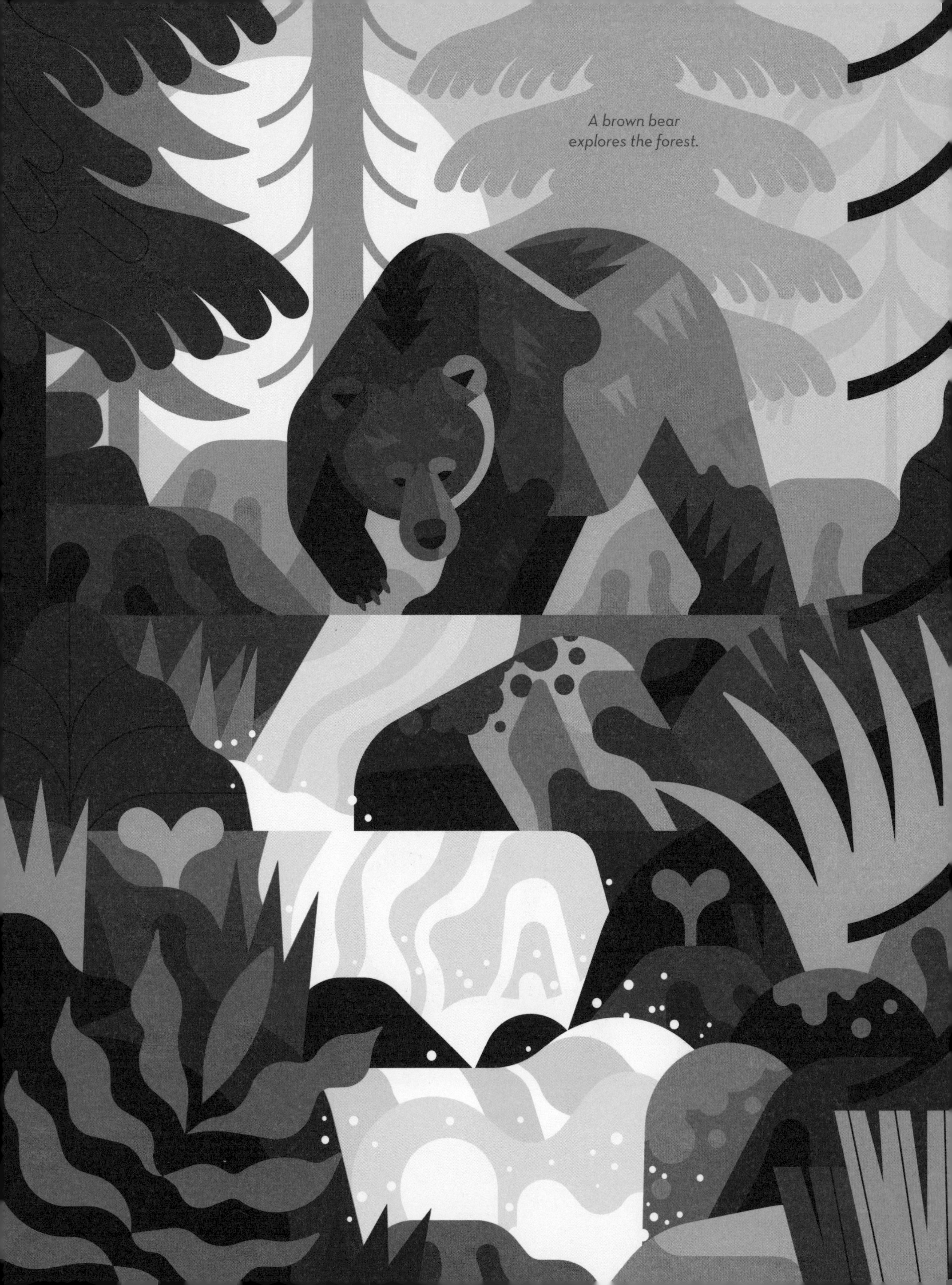

CONTENTS

WHAT ARE BEARS?

Bears are a group of large, powerful mammals with thick fur, big heads, stocky legs, short tails, and small, rounded ears. Today, there are eight distinct species of bear. They can be divided further into subspecies.

Subspecies are groups within a species that are slightly different. They are often defined by where they live, what they eat, how they behave, or how they look, but the most accurate way to define them is their genetic differences. It's not clear how many subspecies there are, but there could more than fifty overall. Two of the most famous examples are grizzlies, an inland subspecies of brown bear, and kodiak bears, a larger island subspecies of brown bear.

This diagram shows the visual differences between black bears and brown bears.

Long ears

Straight face profile

Black bear

Front paw tracks of a black bear

Shoulder hump

Short ears

Sloping bottom

Dished face profile

Brown bear

Front paw tracks of a brown bear

Nom Nom

Bears eat anything from leaves, roots, and berries, to insects, birds, lizards, deer, fish, rodents, and honey, depending on what is available. Giant pandas feed almost entirely on bamboo but given the chance will hunt for small rodents like pika. Bears will also eat carrion (the dead remains of animals killed by other predators) and other bears.

*The diet
of bears*

Home Sweet Home

Bears live in a variety of places, from Arctic sea ice and tundra to mountains, evergreen forests, and tropical jungles. They mainly live in the Northern Hemisphere in Asia, North America, and Europe. Polar bears spend so much of their lives on sea ice that they're actually considered marine mammals.

Now that we've met these hulking great powerhouses, let's climb into their world and get Brainy About Bears!

BY DESIGN

This spectacled bear, named after its distinctive facial markings, showcases many of the special features and abilities for which bears are known.

Brown bear skull

Spectacled bear

Mouth

Bears have an immensely powerful bite due to their massive skulls and strong jaw muscles.

Teeth

Bears have sharp fanglike teeth at the front of their mouths called "canines." These are perfectly shaped weapons for fighting, piercing tough animal hides, and grabbing and killing prey.

Nose

Bears have good eyesight and hearing, but their sense of smell is their primary way of exploring the world. Their expert noses are thought to be the best in the world. In fact, their sense of smell is seven times better than a bloodhound's and 2,100 times better than a human's.

Bears can smell a chocolate bar hidden inside a locked car.

Front Legs

Bears are so powerful that they can move large rocks and fallen tree trunks with ease. They can also swipe at large prey or pull an animal to the ground to make it easier to kill. Although their legs and paws are formidable, they are mostly used for digging up roots and building dens. Their paws are flexible enough to grab fruit and leaves.

Hair

A bear's hair is called its coat. Each coat is made up of thick, short "underfur" and long, shaggy "guard hairs." Their coat keeps bears cosy in winter but can be shed in warmer weather. Hair length can vary from short to very long.

Hind Legs

Bears stand upright on their hind legs (back legs) to look around, fight, or feed. They also stand like this to make themselves look larger and more dangerous when they feel threatened.

A very fluffy sloth bear stands on its hind legs.

The life-size claw of a brown bear

The life-size claw of a black bear

Claws

Bears have five long, non-retractable claws on each paw. Non-retractable claws cannot be withdrawn back into an animal's toes, they are permanently out. They use them to fight, catch prey, dig, and climb.

9

ANCIENT HISTORY

Once upon a time, bears lived in woodlands all over the world. The dawn bear is thought to be the earliest modern bear and lived around 23 to 5.3-million years ago. In comparison, as a species, modern day humans (or *Homo sapiens*) have been around for less than one million years. The dawn bear was the size of a wolf and lived in a very tropical version of Europe. Here are some more bears from the past ...

Although giant short-face bears and cave bears both lived during the Ice Age, they lived on different continents so they never would have crossed paths. Humans, however, would have encountered both species.

Cave Bears

European cave bears were around during the Ice Age. Fossils of the species have mostly been found in caves, implying that they likely spent much more time in caves than modern-day bears. They were roughly the size of the largest modern-day bears and were thought to have a mostly vegetarian diet. Humans are known to have made tools and jewelry out of cave bear bones, and it has been suggested that their skulls may have been used in religious rituals.

Ice Age Bears

The giant short-faced bear had a short, wide snout and has been nicknamed the bulldog bear. It lived during the last Ice Age until 12,000 years ago. Standing on its hind legs, this gigantic, muscular beast would have been more than 9 feet tall, making it one of the largest bears to have ever lived.

Giant short-faced bear

Gladiator helmet

Atlas Bears

Atlas bears are thought to have once been common in North Africa but are now considered extinct. As the Roman Empire colonized the area, people intensively hunted atlas bears and may have used them in their famously brutal gladiatorial fights. Bears were often starved to increase their aggression in the arenas. After the Roman Empire fell, atlas bears were persistently hunted right up until the final one was killed in 1870.

GET A MOVE ON

So how do bears get around? How do they explore their world, find food, and generally get from one place to another? Well, the answer depends on what they're trying to do and where they're trying to do it.

A moon bear (or Asiatic black bear) stands on its hind legs.

Walk the Walk

Okay, walking is a classic. Most humans do it daily. But did you know that some bears can walk on two legs, just like us? This is called "bipedal walking." They can only do this for a few steps and it's not their usual way of walking. Bears usually use all four limbs for their big, powerful, lumbering walk, with their heads swaying from side to side. They use this heavy-set walk because their weight is distributed toward their hind feet, which is also how they can walk upright.

On the Run

Did you know that all bears can sprint? They are all capable of running faster than Olympic sprinters. A single stride of a galloping bear has been measured at 16 feet long! Polar bears quickly overheat when running, but brown bears have been known to run nonstop for 10 miles (although not at the same pace as their short-distance times).

The Malayan sun bear uses its long, curved claws to expertly climb even the smoothest of trees.

Up, Up in a Way

Bears head up trees to eat, rest, escape enemies, play, or hibernate. They use their claws and powerful arms to climb with ease. Even a few of the heaviest grizzly bears can climb, and polar bears are capable of scaling high barriers of ice or rock. Some bears, like the spectacled bear, are so adept at climbing that they sometimes build high-up nests for themselves out of branches and twigs.

A moon bear rests in a nest.

Water Way to Go

Bears like the water. They often wade through it, sit down and splash, float around, hunt for food, discover a new location, or swim just for the pleasure of it. Bears usually swim with a dog-paddle technique and some species can dive below the surface for a while. On dry land, bears shake like a dog to dry out their fur.

A polar bear enjoys a cool, leisurely dip.

MAKING A MEAL OF THINGS

All bears have carnivorous moments once in a while, so how do they catch their prey? Sure, they have powerful paws, crushing jaws, and sharp claws, but it turns out their secret weapon is often just patience and persistence.

During salmon spawning events, there is such an abundance of food that up to ninety grizzlies can crowd together in one location. It's simply too good an opportunity to miss.

Gone Fishing

Fish are an important food source for some species. Brown bears, especially grizzlies, wade in water or wait by rivers and waterfalls in search of fish. In the warmer months, salmon swim upstream in large numbers to lay their eggs in spawning grounds. Bears pounce on the fish as they swim past and stun them. Brown bears can also hook the fish straight out of the water with a swipe of their paw or catch leaping salmon in their teeth. Brown bears can eat up to fifty fish a day.

Big Game

Large bears are capable of bringing down big animals like moose, musk ox, elk, yaks, and bison. Hooves, horns, and antlers can be a powerful deterrent, so bears tend to target young, injured, or distracted animals as prey. The easier the hunt, the greater the chance of success. Bears stalk their prey catlike, rush at it, and then pounce. This is known as "ambushing."

A grizzly bear targets a healthy adult elk while it crosses through a stream.

Whack-A-Hole

Ringed seals make up the vast majority of a polar bear's diet. Seals spend a lot of their time under water hunting fish, but eventually have to come to the surface to breathe. They build and maintain air holes in the ice for this purpose. Polar bears can smell seals more than half a mile away and have been known to wait by a seal's breathing hole for hours (even days) for one to pop up. Although polar bears spend half their lives in search of food, less than two percent of their hunts are successful.

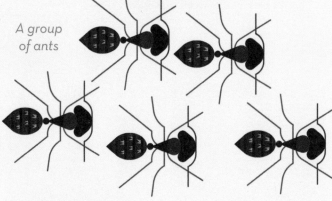

A group of ants

A squirrel buries its nuts.

Ground Work

Bears don't just eat big meals. Grizzly bears will happily eat mice and grasshoppers, or devour a line of passing ants. Sloth bears can locate grubs three feet deep in soil, then use their long snout and lips to vacuum out their prey.

What a Steal

Sometimes bears just steal food. They commonly scavenge kills or seek out food caches sourced by other animals. In the Rocky Mountains, red squirrels bury whitebark pine nuts for a future meal. Grizzly bears in the area happily sniff out these bounties and chow down. Poor squirrels.

ANTISOCIAL LIFE

Bears are shy and tend to spend most of their lives alone, usually avoiding interactions with other bears. They are not generally territorial animals and don't defend areas from other bears. Instead, they have a sense of personal space and try to stay away from one another. But bears will inevitably meet each other in the wild, so what happens then?

Leave Your Mark

Roughly ninety percent of the ways bears communicate involves scent. They use scratching, biting, rubbing, peeing, and pooping to show other bears where they've been. Males (known as boars) tend to scent more than females (known as sows). Pandas even have a special gland near their bottom that they use to leave a waxy substance on trees, and their tails are used to spray pee farther.

A giant panda is leaving hairs and scent on this tree with the bonus of having a nice back scratch.

Bear Necessities

Bears form hierarchies based on size, age, health, confidence, and experience. These hierarchies are social positions that determine who is in charge of a situation and who needs to back away. Fights between bears can have serious consequences, so figuring out who is boss in a nonviolent way is in everyone's best interest. Large old boars or sows with offspring tend to be the most dominant.

Power Moves

To be as intimidating as possible, bears may stand up to exaggerate their size, strut toward each other with their shoulders high, stare, or display their muzzle and teeth. Large boars sometimes roar to scare their opponents, and others may have to resort to wrestling, biting, and swiping at each other with their immense forelimbs. When the winner is decided, the loser may turn sideways, lower their head, or sit or lie down to show they know their place.

Two adult polar bears battle it out to decide who's in charge.

TAKE A REST

Some bears sleep and rest for several months in regions with cold winters. They don't "hibernate" in this time but they enter a lighter state of sleep, called "torpor." Similar to hibernation, they lower their body temperature, how much they breathe, and even how fast their hearts beat. While hibernation can last for several days, weeks, or months, torpor happens in short bursts, sometimes only for a night. Essentially, it is a super-deep sleep that helps them to conserve energy.

During torpor, the black bear's heart rate can slow from fifty-five beats per minute to just nine.

Getting Comfy

During the winter months, bears will wake up to move around, groom themselves, and get comfortable again. If the winter has a warm spell, the bear may even walk around outside, but it will always remain close to the den. Only brown bears, American black bears, Asiatic black bears, and pregnant polar bears will den for winter.

Fed Up

There is less food available in cold winters, so to prepare to enter their dens for a few months, bears eat and gain as much weight as they can. This excess-feeding is called "hyperphagia." Sows may double their weight during the summer and fall months. Some bears can eat up to 40,000 calories a day, which is roughly sixteen times more than the recommended amount for an adult human male.

A black bear's den

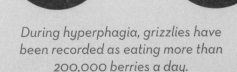

During hyperphagia, grizzlies have been recorded as eating more than 200,000 berries a day.

You've Made Your Bed, Now Lie In It

Bears use natural shelters like caves and logs as their dens or will simply dig out the soil for a ground den. Finding a secure and secret location for a den is their primary concern. The dens usually have an entrance, a tunnel, and a chamber. The chamber may be lined with leaves, sand, and grass as bedding.

Ignoring Nature's Call

Bears in the coldest regions can go into torpor for up to seven months in their dens. In such an enclosed space, you can imagine why it might not be smart to leave your pee and poop everywhere. Bears don't tend to eat, drink, or pass any waste during torpor. A weird side effect to this is that bears create a fecal plug. This is a poop that doesn't come out immediately, and slowly dries out and hardens as the moisture is absorbed back into the bear's body. When spring comes around, bears finally poop it out near the entrance to their den.

BORN THIS WAY

Some female bears will give birth in the den during torpor. Baby bears are called cubs. Despite being some of the largest land predators on the planet, cubs start life as small, toothless creatures that are unable to hear, smell, or see, and are only covered in a few fine hairs. It can take a month and a half for some bear cubs to open their eyes for the first time.

A newborn baby panda only weighs the same as a deck of cards. It is 900 times smaller than its mother.

Milking It

Newborn cubs rely on their mother's milk for food. This is called "nursing." While spectacled bears typically nurse for only eight weeks, sloth bears may nurse for up to two years! Bear milk in colder regions can be around ten times fattier than that of humans, and polar bear milk is so thick that it looks more like condensed milk (and smells like fish). This rich diet is perfect for building the strength of these would-be hunters.

Family Life

Mothers are solely responsible for raising bear cubs. Males are nowhere to be seen and are thought of as a threat. Bear mothers, however, are devoted to their cubs and make very attentive teachers and fierce protectors. Bear families stay close together for safety, since cubs are at risk from predators, including other bears. When necessary, grizzly and brown bear sows may carry a cub by putting its whole head in their mouth. Most species allow cubs to have a ride on their back.

Sloth bear cubs ride on their mother's back by clinging onto her fur with their paws.

Child's Play

Cubs have a lot to learn before adulthood and play is an extremely important part of their education. Bears often play right up into adulthood, but this is usually done alone. As cubs, bears have been seen wrestling together, splashing water, boxing, sliding on ice, pouncing, chasing each other, hiding, shoving their sibling, playing tug-of-war, rolling down hills, making snowballs, and teasing monkeys.

Two polar bear cubs play-fighting.

LITTLE AND LARGE

Featured Creatures: Polar Bears

Polar bears are the largest species of bear, and the largest meat-eating land animal on Earth. The largest recorded polar bear weighed more than one ton and was nearly twelve feet long, which is over twice the height of the average adult human.

Cold

Polar bears are only found in the Arctic, a snow-covered area around the North Pole, where temperatures can drop to an incredible -95ºF. Polar bears rely on the sea ice to travel and hunt. Arctic ice is continually melting, refreezing, and moving with the ocean currents, so a polar bear's habitat is constantly changing.

A life-size illustration of a polar bear's head

On the Road Again

Polar bears need to keep moving in order to find food. They can go several months without eating anything but when they finally find a meal, they eat as much of it as they can. Large male polar bears are capable of hunting walruses, dolphins, belugas, and narwhals but usually stick to seals and seal pups.

White Fur

Polar bears are white, right? Nope. Their skin is black and their coat is actually made up of hairs that are colorless hollow tubes that just look white when they reflect light.

Featured Creatures: Sun Bears

Sun bears are the smallest species of bear. Some adults weigh roughly the same as a boxer dog and reach less than three feet in height. In English, they are named after their patch of golden fur on their chests, but in Malaysia, where some sun bears are native, their name means "he who likes to sit high." Sun bears are the most arboreal species of bear, meaning that they spend a lot of their lives in trees.

A life-size illustration of a sun bear's head

TO SCALE

Here is a line-up of large bears from each species, standing next to a 5'5"
tall person. Boars are generally larger than sows, so this is a page of males.

Black bear

Sun bear

Giant panda

Sloth bear

Polar bear

Spectacled bear

Human

Moon bear

Kodiak (brown) bear

Kodiak bears are the largest subspecies of brown bear. They are isolated to the islands of the Kodiak Archipelago in Alaska. The largest ever recorded Kodiak bear was only slightly smaller and lighter than the largest polar bear.

10 inches

AND THE AWARD GOES TO...

Brown bears are the fastest running bears. Using their enormously powerful front legs, they can bound along at speeds of 35 mph, roughly 7.5 mph faster than the human world record.

The highly coveted award for the longest tail compared to body size, goes to ... the panda bear! Most animals use their tails for balance, stability, or even picking things up, but for bears, they are just a furry flap of skin covering their bottom. This may seem funny, but nature's underpants can help protect bears' bottoms from both weather conditions and from nasty parasites.

Polar bears are the best swimmers in the bear family. They use their massive, slightly webbed paws to paddle great distances between ice. A female polar bear was recorded swimming for nine straight days, covering a whopping 408 miles of water. During that time, she lost nearly a quarter of her bodyweight. In the past, polar bears didn't have to swim so far but due to climate change, the sea ice is melting, making these epic journeys more commonplace.

Despite being the smallest in the group, sun bears are thought to have the largest claws. Their extremely long, curved claws on their front paws grow to more than four inches in length and are used to rip open trees, termite nests, and hives.

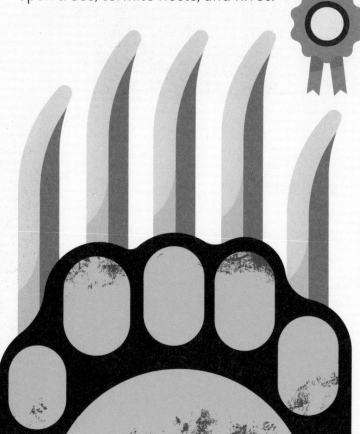

Sun bears also walk away with the award for the longest tongue. At a massive 10 inches, it is used to collect insects, pupae, larvae, eggs, and honey from hard-to-reach places inside nests and hives. Bees and wasps sting their attacker in defense, but to a sun bear, it's worth the trouble to collect their sweet prize.

Polar bears also swipe the award for the best divers. Polar bears dive to find seaweed, catch fish, hunt seabirds, or even ambush seals resting on ice platforms. One polar bear was recorded holding its breath for more than three minutes while stalking seals.

LIVING WITH BEARS

Bears are large, powerful predators and they can be a danger to local human populations, crops, and livestock. Bear attacks are rare but often highlighted in the media. It's important to remember that even when a bear hurts a human, kills an animal, or takes food from a farmer, it is not evil or cruel for doing so. Bears do not kill for pleasure. They are opportunistic predators that only kill for food or in self-defense. They take crops because they are a readily available food source.

A bear living close to humans can figure out that it can get an easy meal by scavenging from their trash. Once a resource like this is discovered, they will return to it, which can be dangerous for the humans and the bear. Polar bears tend to be some of the most curious and aggressive of bears because of how hungry they get. In locations where food sources are high, and there is sufficient hunting space, there is less need for a bear to wander into the world of humans.

Stay Safe

Bear attacks on humans are rare, but they do happen. Usually it is when a bear has been startled, when they are looking for or defending food, or when they are protecting their cubs. They would prefer to scare you off or run away, rather than fight, but if they do attack, it can have tragic consequences.

The best way to keep you and the bears safe, is to avoid encounters with them. Areas with wild bears usually share advice on how to stay safe, based on the species and the time of year. It's important to read the advice and follow any instructions they give. For example, in North America and Canada, it is recommended that you don't walk alone, you stick to walking trails and you make lots of noise to let bears know you're there. If a bear can hear you coming from a long way off, they will usually head in the opposite direction. It is also important to stay alert to signs of bears including tracks, turned-over logs, poop, or killed prey. If you see any of these signs, head back the way you came.

A sow with cubs will attack anything that gets too close to her cubs.

BEAR MYTHOLOGY

Bears have been feared, revered, and worshipped by numerous cultures around the world for thousands of years. They have been considered spirits, immortal beings, gods, religious symbols, ancestors, healers, messengers, or guides and nearly always treated with great respect. Some cultures believed that it was bad luck to call a bear by its name in case it angered the bear spirits, so they gave them alternate names meaning "Owner of the Earth" or "Masters of the Forest" instead.

Ukuku

In the Peruvian Andes, ukukus are trickster half-human, half-bears with supernatural strength. During the traditional Quyllurit'i festival, performers dressed as ukukus climb a glacier to cut blocks of ice and bring them back to the people. Once melted, the sacred water was thought to have medicinal qualities and purify the people. Due to climate change, this ritual is no longer practiced.

The Great Bear

Ursa Major, or the Great Bear, is one of the most famous constellations in the northern sky. A constellation is a group of stars visible at night that are recognizable as a picture. This clump of stars look like a large bear, and many northern cultures have given it a title with the same meaning. A prehistoric myth about it, known as the Cosmic Hunt, tells of a bear being wounded by hunters and then transforming into the constellation. Another nearby constellation is known as Ursa Minor, or the Little Bear.

Ungnyeo

In this creation myth, a tiger and a bear wish to become human. A divine king tells them to wait in a cave for 100 days, eating only garlic and plants. The tiger leaves but the bear remains inside until she is transformed into a bear woman. Ungnyeo (the bear woman) marries the divine king and they have a son, who becomes the founder of Korea.

Berserkers

According to Old Norse sagas, some Viking warriors wore bear skins without armor and fought in a trance-like fury. These "Berserkers" supposedly foamed at the mouth, howled like animals, and gnawed at their own shields. They were said to draw superhuman strength from the bear and became immune to sharp weapons and fire. Some interpretations imply that the warriors actually shape-shifted into bears during battle. Today, the word *berserk* is used to mean angry and wild.

I'LL HAVE THE VEGETARIAN OPTION, PLEASE

Featured Creatures: Giant Panda

The giant panda is an iconic animal with a lovably clumsy demeanor and unique black-and-white markings. They eat almost exclusively bamboo in the wild, despite not having the correct bacteria in their guts to process it properly. It is such an inefficient process that less than a third of the bamboo they eat is properly digested. They must eat up to a quarter of their own bodyweight and spend up to sixteen hours each day munching their food.

Bamboo is a tough, grasslike plant that grows very quickly and can reach 100 feet high. Pandas love to eat the leaves of bamboo, which makes them a special type of herbivore called a "folivore." Giant pandas even have a special wrist bone, which acts a bit like a thumb, to help them grasp clumps of bamboo to feed.

Scientists have worked out that adult pandas need to find a lot of bamboo to survive. Through deforestation and human developments, there are few areas that can support this appetite. Until recently, giant pandas were listed as an endangered species, restricted to isolated strips of land too far apart to travel between. This caused further problems to their already slow breeding habits. Through intensive conservation efforts, including breeding programs and the protection and linking of critical habitats, wild panda numbers are on the rebound but they are still classed as a vulnerable species.

Pandas are unable to hibernate because they cannot gain enough weight through their bamboo diet.

33

PAWS FOR THOUGHT

Polar bears and giant pandas have become the poster animals for the effects of climate change and the urgent need for greater conservation. Iconic photos of polar bears struggling to find enough sea ice, and stories of pandas refusing to breed, are commonplace. These two species serve as constant reminders of the damage we do to the planet and show us the direct consequences of human behaviors.

Panda to the Masses

Giant pandas are known as an "umbrella species." Conservation efforts to preserve their beloved bamboo forest may indirectly benefit other species that share the habitat, including other vulnerable and endangered animals like the snub-nosed monkey and snow leopard. The charisma and charm of the panda appeals to large audiences and encourages support for greater habitat conservation, giving more opportunities to others around it.

On Thin Ice

It is proven that human activity is the reason for our oceans, land, and atmosphere heating up. The last decade has been the warmest period in the last 125,000 years. That may sound nice for a few days at the beach, but this heat is causing us to lose 1.2 trillion tons of ice each year, which makes both the Earth's temperature and our sea levels rise even quicker. All of this is bad news for the planet's future, but many animals are feeling the effects right now. Seals, a polar bear's primary food source, rely on sea ice for raising their pups. It is likely that as sea ice decreases, more polar bears will starve and sadly, polar bears may soon face extinction in the wild.

What Can We Do?

As the children of today grow older, they will shape the future of humanity and our role in conservation and climate action. Maybe you will become a lawyer, politician, company-owner, scientist, engineer, climatologist, creator, or community leader with influence over how others choose to treat the planet. Maybe people like you will one day be able to prioritize and protect the health and safety of bears and their habitats for generations to come.

A sloth bear snacking on a line of ants.

INDEX

*Subspecies of Black bear

** Subspecies of Brown bear

Collect the whole About Animals series

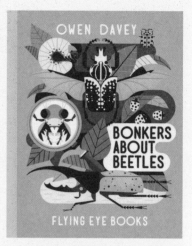

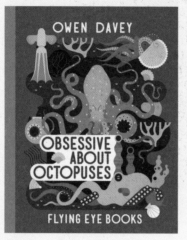
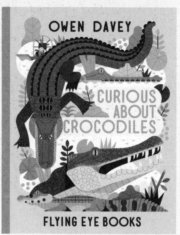
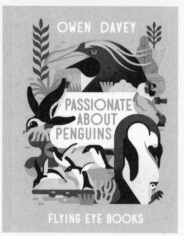

For my youngest cub, Robyn.

First edition published in 2024 by Flying Eye Books Ltd.
27 Westgate Street, London, E8 3RL.

Text and illustrations © Owen Davey 2024

Owen Davey has asserted his right under the
Copyright, Designs and Patents Act, 1988, to be identified
as the Author and Illustrator of this Work.

Every attempt has been made to ensure any statements written as fact have been checked
to the best of our abilities. However, we are still human, thankfully, and occasionally
little mistakes may crop up. Should you spot any errors, please email info@flyingeyebooks.net.

Edited by Sara Forster and Kate Birch
Designed by Sarah Crookes
Scientific consultant: Teague Stubbington

1 3 5 7 9 10 8 6 4 2

Published in the US by Flying Eye Books Ltd.
Printed in Poland on FSC® certified paper.

MIX
Paper | Supporting
responsible forestry
FSC
www.fsc.org   FSC® C163799

ISBN: 978-1-83874-879-1
www.flyingeyebooks.com